**YOU
BREAK IT
YOU
BUY IT**

ESSENTIAL POETS SERIES 304

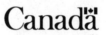

ONTARIO ARTS COUNCIL
CONSEIL DES ARTS DE L'ONTARIO

an Ontario government agency
un organisme du gouvernement de l'Ontario

Canada Council   Conseil des arts
for the Arts   du Canada

Guernica Editions Inc. acknowledges the support of
the Canada Council for the Arts and the Ontario Arts Council.
The Ontario Arts Council is an agency of the Government of Ontario.

We acknowledge the financial support of the Government of Canada.

LYNN TAIT

YOU
BREAK IT
YOU
BUY IT

GUERNICA
EDITIONS

TORONTO • CHICAGO • BUFFALO • LANCASTER (U.K.)
2023

Guernica Founder: Antonio D'Alfonso

Michael Mirolla, editor
Cover and interior design: Rafael Chimicatti
Cover image: Simon Lee / Unsplash

Guernica Editions Inc.
287 Templemead Drive, Hamilton, (ON), Canada L8W 2W4
2250 Military Road, Tonawanda, N.Y. 14150-6000 U.S.A.
www.guernicaeditions.com

Distributors:
University of Toronto Press Distribution (UTP)
5201 Dufferin Street, Toronto (ON), Canada M3H 5T8
Independent Publishers Group (IPG)
814 N Franklin Street, Chicago, IL 60610, U.S.A

First edition.
Printed in Canada.

Legal Deposit – Third Quarter
Library of Congress Catalogue Card Number: 2023935350
Library and Archives Canada Cataloguing in Publication
Title: You break it you buy it / Lynn Tait.
Names: Tait, Lynn, 1956- author.
Series: Essential poets ; 304.
Description: Series statement: Essential poets series ; 304 | Poems.
Identifiers: Canadiana 2023021116X | ISBN 9781771838108 (softcover)
Classification: LCC PS8589.A347 Y68 2023 | DDC C811/.6—dc23

To my son Stephen – my beautiful Falstaff
The love, the laughter, we will remember

and Adele – I miss our afternoons.

Sandra Lawrence, who saw a creative little girl,

and to my husband and best friend, Rob,
who still loves me madly.

Contents

I. Disconnections

II. The Enemies We Cannot See

III. Collision Course

I.
Disconnections

He Wants a Dangerous Poem

for Patrick Lane

What does he mean?
Confess my sins on paper?
Open a vein? Terrorize the public?
Plant traps between lines?
Throw bombs after each period?

Write about leaving home at sixteen?
Carrying hash for my boyfriend?
(The one time the cops stop me,
they confiscate a box of tampons.)

Dangerous, as in fear of the almost, the close call:
the loss of sanity, life savings, husband, child?

Don't think I've done anything dangerous lately.
Is this my year for living dangerously?

When I think about it,
people can be dangerous.
Well, maybe more confusing,
a wearing down or out.
O the times I've almost bitten
off my lips, ripped imaginary duct tape
off my mouth, or struggled to keep it on—
that's kind of dangerous isn't it?

Probably more painful,
like sitting up all night
writing with a pencil by flashlight,
inside an eco-friendly lodge
in the middle of nowhere,
fighting off insects,
thinking this is the stupidest
fucking thing I've ever written,
and the only real danger:
losing my mind while writing this poem.
And the bugs, the damn bugs.

Now We Are Six

after poets Robin Richardson, Kate Rogers,
Catherine Owen, Pooh, Piglet and me

Met them all in the flesh,
soft encounters and hard copy.

Connected, computed and measured each other's days,
commented on men, women, relationships, travel.

Been flash-framed, cut-away, pushed-over;
our sets change with whoever's storefront mannequin
is displayed—clothing optional.

We've ridden the backs of creatures
that could tear us apart to the beat
of a Joni Mitchell song.

A fish can't whistle and neither can I.
Trying to spoon June—she says,
you're just not a good fit.

Don't judge a poet by her age or her eye-liner.
We're all Goddesses circumventing the globe.
Within our social media we settle for unrest with sunshine.

Now we are six,
caught in a corona, the same bedroom,
same curtains, different nightmares:

Dragons replace flowers,
angry mother cuts me into squares.
Her mother bakes me into rounds, sews me shut.

My family tree—French not Russian,
but we've all branched out to keep the peace,
our bodies grafted onto the desires of men.

We sit the way we want.
I'll spread myself apart for a dozen oysters, raw.
The wine—saved for dinner.

One lazy eye sets me up as drunkard—
another unforgiving body part.
Our flesh betrays us.
Our scars: poetry.

"Strip"

"Mother takes off her belt
orders me to STRIP."

Such a naked word.
It's the hissing sound of cruelty
the reek of dead forests and seedy carnivals
the taste of sulfur
secrets hidden under sandpaper.

No matter what the context
the word snaps
and I shudder.

It sticks in the throat—
a fly trap soiling itself with festering buzz-words
disturbs the drone of afternoon aircraft during nap time
when flowers on the curtains change shape
and move at my command.

It erases like a sudden sandstorm
blasting through rock
eroding great wonders.

It is a tortuous sound
a humiliation
proving the punishment
never fits the crime.

Horse Hair

When a child I dreamt of growing my hair long.
Locks carried by the wind, a horse's mane.
I'd gallop, jump fences, rear up
queen of the plains, sun filtering through long tresses,
rushing along beaches, salt scent flaring my nostrils,
curls loose and full of sea.

As my hair lengthened,
I measured the distance of strands
around face to mouth where locks
barely touching lips might open,
waves might crash upon the shores
of oceans rising out of deserts.

Instead, a tide sucked back
leaving an empty basin.

Grandmother always takes it upon herself
to snip it short and straight, curls tamed,
reins tightened.

Mother is angry. Fancies me groomed professionally.
Grandma beats her out of the gate every time.
They both jockey for the same position:
keeping this magnificent beast shackled,
away from any surge of waves, confined,
tethered to maternal posts of iron wills.

No Certificate Can Explain Me

I arrived on a Monday, birthed from one canal
to a cold, smooth, grey world, light
bending to a particulate blue.

In time, I became a wound,
too many colours for one woman.

Painted into a corner,
not passing through anything without her approval,
all chromatic wheels at my disposal
spin off their axis in all the wrong shades.

She refused to answer questions or articulate secrets,
my arrival almost virginal
photographic evidence erased,
paternal ancestral tree axed,
scorched earth policy in effect.
Who was the enemy?

Please, let the unsaid speak to me.
Not sure I'm an official document of a bright anyone.
Birth certificate of hidden identities
stamped non-negotiable, passport confiscated,

I passed through her and should have kept going,
pushing through grey corners, splitting blue walls,
diving into green.

Before Meeting My Cousin for the First Time, or Waking Up After All These Years

to my cousin Donnie, and my father, whom I never met.

… there are openings in our lives of which we know nothing
     —Jane Hirshfield

My cousin, my father, a woman, and I
are sitting in a stairwell.
We are eating sandwiches.
I know the two men in this dream,
though we've never met.

The woman is my mother—
she won't shut up,
that's the first clue.
I tell her to be quiet, but
she's mad I'm spending time
with these two men. They ignore her,
so I do too, her constant annoying drone.

The scowl on her face I've seen before,
that's the second clue.
The men and I talk to each other
as if she's not there.
We eat our sandwiches
as if she's not there.
I wake up not knowing
how the dream ends.

The day before I meet my cousin for the first time,
my uncle and I visit my mother.
She doesn't talk much anymore,
doesn't recognize us.
Says her head hurts, and falls asleep.
Next day, I meet my cousin.
For the first time,
I see pictures of my father.

It's the day, I wake up—
find out we were all held captive
by the woman in the dream,
the woman who never stopped talking.

Clutter

For as long as she can remember,
couldn't hear her own voice, only Mother's.
Molded, kilned to remain small,
dusted off, brought out for show
but never placed well,
display-cased in cartoonish muted hues,
groomed to perform feats ill-prepared for,
a joke with its own laugh track.

She remained on shelves in curio cupboards
alongside knick-knacks, paddy-whacks
someone stole the bone,
hand-crafted, sanded, varnished with guilt,
shame or regret—take your pick.

She's a children's book with missing pages,
an aging box of broken records,
wind-up curiosity clashing tinny patina cymbals,
tiny figure in a doll house, nursery empty,

found in messy second-hand shops,
propped up next to tea animals,
painted ladies in bone china splendour,
trinket amid a cast of a thousand odds and ends.

There she is!
Hair-line-cracked mosaic everyone points at
with eyes glazed as pottery;
held, examined, set back—
never in the same spot,
usually slightly askew
before they move on.
There's so much more to see.

Some day she'll be newspaper-wrapped
in obsolete ads from 2012,
holed up in basements indefinitely, settling
into cardboard ill-suited for flood or drought.

Frozen

Cemeteries are now my home away from home.
We celebrate our son's birth, his death—
a shot of tequila on site.

When in Toronto I visit a family of graves.
Father, aunts, grandparents, I never knew.
Does our son recognize their spirits?

My parents were pieces from different puzzles.
Mother lived in a world of disappointment—
no one fulfilling her demand to be adored.

Scooped the life out of three husbands and me;
wrapped up our most valued morsels,
stashed us separately in cold storage,
together preserved in a forever freezer burn.

She wore the word *Mother* like a badge,
a manipulating incantation on
answering machines: *Lynn, it's your Mother*.
The when of conversations—
the only control I had.

My biological father was the missing piece,
stuck in radio silence, our transmissions
not strong enough to cut through
her information black-outs.

His best friend's kids were substitutes.
When we finally all met they told me
I was loved. Imagine—loved in absentia.

I never knew what he looked like until my late 50's.
He'd passed by then—alone with bottled regrets—
our fear of rejecting one another choked us
like a leash held tightly our entire lives.
No idea I looked at him for 29 years
through the face of his grandson.

Crash Landings

Mother is blue-pink, a thin paper kite collapsed,
crushing into herself, found in places
she can't recall.

Asleep, she is body-grounded, fetus-bound.
Awake, her head above clouds: loop de loop compliments,
demands, clever humour depending on the moment,
dangerous one minute, flailing the next, back to sleep.

Light catches her skin, a transparency
we saw years ago when she swooped,
dive-bombed us, blaming the wind
for all horrific crashes, her failure to remain aloft.

A life spent above a wilderness she refused to see.
Her desire to control thermals, self-inflicted holding
pattern—
one breeze away—an almost sentient being
who removed her heart from her sky,
burned through both string and tail.

Force of nothing,
caught in a whirlwind without bright edges
calls out—*help   help me,* in a sudden gust of fear.
She wants me to take her home.

How did this see-through weightless woman
cause so much damage? This frail being,
led by sudden bursts of ego, changed lives
with a single line, one flick of her tail.

She's fallen from the sky so many times
spine and ribs remain coiled and bent.
There is no smooth landing,
no hint of a soaring end.

When Mother Passed

I wasn't there and was glad of it.
She remained in this world three years too long,
as if God said: *Yes Lynn, three more years you
can handle, I have her for eternity.*
He was in no hurry to receive her.

Mother existed three hours away.
From an early age we were worlds apart.
My name and place in her life erased when in her nineties,
visits at the home went from pleasantries,
to sour silence,
sullen stare of no trust,
a hiss coming out of her eyes.

After her death, the memorial: a family scramble
hodgepodge of events more pressing.
A month later, not everyone showed—
an extra thinning of bodies at graveside,
the importance of elsewhere.

We are invited to share a memory.
Silence closed around us like a coffin
the five of us hard pressed to think of joy on the spot.
My eldest cousin recalls my mother yelling at her.
We all laughed—
Too many stones. Not enough rainbows.

Slipstream

> *We are all made up fragments, so shapelessly and strangely assembled that every moment, every piece plays its own game. And there is as much difference between ourselves and ourselves as between us and others.*
>   —Montaigne

We drift into various life forms,
enter unnoticed through separate doors,
assume the shape of masks,
stained-glass and candles
so we might see ourselves aflame,
reflect on our ability to grow soft and small,
provide light to fit and fuse harlequin elements—
pieces of persona contoured and shaded.

Avoiding liaisons black with holes,
we shift into sound waves,
gain access to conversations
clinging to the sides of diphthongs
that drop dangerous and sudden
into hard letters, unsigned, cut short—
each long sound bears with it an uncomfortable silence,
no one able to comment on our painful transitions,
the energy needed to sustain each form.

When time permits,
we cover ourselves with moss
to soften the violence of flight,
listen for ripples in the atmosphere
waiting for the proper slipstream
to carry us, back to the place
where a slight turn of our head
altered the course of planets.

Theories on Fair-Weather Friends

They're like silly dogs in china shops;
know their manners when it suits them.
Tails wagging, hide under sofas,
refuse to come out and face their messes,
chewed hands strewn about, pieces
of people they've lost interest in,

or

maybe they're swamp-things masquerading
as cool, mysterious pools—can't see the muck
until you venture in; when the heat turns up
you're hit with a drying stench,

or

maybe they're like card players,
sitting in the bush—when least expected,
trump their partner's Ace.

Maybe we give them too much credit.

Maybe they're just unhappy,
fearing their own irreverence.
Irrelevance? Maybe, both.
They'll deny it either way,

or

maybe they're dying cacti, blanched-out
green thorns split at the top,
porous deadwood inside,

or,

maybe all the above, depending on
the time of day or their blood sugar levels.

Who Could Try to Tell Us We're Not Beautiful?

Does it start in play group, schoolyard?
All the hair-pulling:
our first act of violence.
Gossip—
the poison of the passed note,
the cupped hand in a whispered text of venom.

No valentines for you.
You can't play with us
metal mouth, four eyes, faggot,
retard. You've got cooties

graduates to an afterhours coffee clutch,
playground grown-ups writing off
who's no longer worthy.

Oh, the buzz!
Frightened by the beauty they lack,
prepared to sting their pain on you,
spit out—
take this anger, this anguish—it's yours.
But it's not.

When Geese Cry Wolf

Webs of feet race towards
their offbeat honks for help.
Alarmed by the colour of my wings
mandibles click-click

and at least two will follow.
They'll team up
but mostly gaggle about,

honk in unison, paddle
in sour puddles, self-made.
Mistaking eggs for canine droppings,

race-waddle in flock-fear
certain my feathers are fur.
After territorial squawking, fits
of hissing far longer than necessary,

peck themselves silly,
hoot-howl in mud at the moon,
claim I'm a demon—
my wings—teeth on fire.

Crossing Lines or O Brother,
Here Comes the Sisterhood

Told her how my nose was broken years ago
courtesy of her friend.
She offers: *He probably doesn't remember.*
Three year drama / cut—that's a wrap!
An early 70's relationship similar to
Bonnie and Clyde's machine-gunned car,
riddled instead with sex, drugs, rock and roll.

When I learn he's in the program,
wondered if I'd get that 12 step apology.
He always was brilliantly weak.
I seem to do well with forgiveness;
the forgetting's a slippery slope
—his female friends: riddled with men
shooting us up with alibis.

We don't have to be on any spectrum to misread intentions.
I've always been a hot messy princess
feeling that pea wedged in my back,
no mattress necessary.

Someone's sister says I look too comfortable around men.
She's probably right. Once you deal with women
whose actions slide sideways
you get a feel for mind fucks.
I crave simplicity in connections:
less wires sticking into me, the better.

Men—cut out all that red tape.
I can unravel their Christmas lights,
trip their wires,
ascertain their plus and minuses,
pull their plugs; extinguish those lights
in a single swipe of my little hand.

My own kind: complicated challenges for any sisterhood,
board games you can't win or tie,
snakes without ladders, games
where it's safer in jail or hitching rides
on the railway; risking life and reputation
we twirl fortune's wheel insisting on re-spins
until the world tilts in our direction.

Snake Bites

You raise yourself up,
    appearing larger than you really are,
        coil around your wine glass
          and spit from across the room.
        That willingness to share what you
      don't understand quick-nips ankles
      tattooed with tainted ideas.
  Henna-hued swirls intertwine,
not Celtic looking,
nothing exotic—
  more like smoke trails
    travelling the leg; and beyond
      your scaled-down version
       of a well-fed viper
        fork-tongued and smiling—
       you hope I choke
     on my own venom.

After a Tall Drink with the Short-Sighted

And though she be but little, she is fierce.
            —*A Midsummer Night's Dream,* Shakespeare

Lord knows I see red the moment someone calls me *cute.*
The fire ignites in a flash fuelled by *cute* little sticks,
but I keep it to myself. No one is interested
in what this little elf has to say.

No one—that's a little over the top, like self as elf
bounding over the flames in my brain,
sailing over the slow burn with a smirk
that says it knows more than it lets on.

Little but fierce by age ten,
taller at thirty than now,
with shrinkage comes wisdom.
Smoldering past senior moments

I'm dismissed by these strange beings—
itching to pat me on the head.
My baby blues roll like dice turning up snake eyes
on a table I can barely see over.

My intensity filters through comedy routines,
my self-absorbed life, *cute* little feet up,
cute little audience in a world of vaudeville,

a*cutely* aware—actors falling all over themselves
fighting to get on stage, yanking
on doors of opportunity without knocking.

I don't want to tell people what to do,
but you seldom get through doors
big head first. But what do I know?

I slipped though the keyhole hours ago.

To Whom This May Concern

I recommend you consolidate your views,
then, send me a memo
outlining your decision
as to my emotional whereabouts.

Map out plans
for my continuous downhill slide;
place and connect pins in black and white
representing personality place markers
informing me of all my recent issues.

Send me monthly notifications
regarding my shortcomings;
include a brief description of each
so I may act accordingly.

Prepare a database
of all my communication problems,
an up-dateable list of mixed signals.
Make note of every quiet pause
alive with meaning,
every word's hidden agenda
bursting with questionable intentions.

Present, with full citations,
everything I should have done,
should not have said.
Plot a course of action
based on these assumptions.

Place all data on a statistical graph;
draft a paper outlining
how my negative trend
will affect you in the next six months.
File it under S for scapegoat.

The Guitar Shredder's Ex:
Non Sequitur in E Minor

I've made my share of messes—
like one white duck on your wall
my feathers pinned to the fridge,
a chick magnet twittering characters
into cyberspace, amped up with donnybrooks
and plain old-fashioned bullshit.

I'm not sliding
into that song and dance routine anymore.
There's enough fake news out there
I know a victim when I hear one, and you're not it.

Yeah, I could sing the blues.
I'm over-extended across
twelve bars but can see
through your muddy waters.

Hand on my neck,
bending my strings,
on a scale from one to ten reach
a solid pentatonic five. In this new age
of gospel truth

are you open to minor suggestions?
Now that your playlist includes philosophy,
belting out fallacies without a song sheet—
all your sharps turn flat.

You could always improvise.
But don't get too close.
Once straw men burst into flames
there's nothing left to support your conclusions—
but I hear there's a tonic for that.

Rain

God's in a pissing contest.
    Under the pressure
        of a full bladder,
            his keg has sprung a leak.
                You're soaking it in as it takes you away.

Naked lady
    curled up in a massive martini glass
        waves at you,
            olive bobble dances around her.
            She appears shaken
not stirred.

You're running up a tab.
    No crease between rain-soaked sheets,
        ironed flat on your back
            you'll spread your legs
                for an angel's kiss and free tapas,
but any kickshaw will do.

A Change in Travel Plans

You've saddled me with a lie I never deserved.
You led me to believe I was responsible.
—Irving Wallace, *The Prize*

Like travel agents
planning a client's itinerary,
the two of them discuss how
she's a train wreck waiting to happen.

Checking off old wounds,
pray mine open,
so theirs might close—
hearts and minds packed deep inside locked luggage
they prepare for a monotonous trip
in the wrong direction.

On my rails, windows reflect a silver scene.
Landmarks come and go,
weeping willows glisten with loss,
baptized in sorrow's dew,
soaked up by roots of joy;
there's laughter in the leaves, thunder
and despite odd days of rain—love.

I'm not waiting for an apology.
I've left their battlefield.
Hiding beneath each other's armoured skirts—
does it smell like victory under there?

I have few regrets.
My heart hums in my hands.
The runaway train
they're counting on
is just around the bend.
But I'm not on it.

Our True Friends

We don't deserve them.
Our offerings we think:
too small or offering nothing at all.

Yet, we're inundated with their invisible bonds,
love and the names of hearts
who spend countless hours as ears,
shoulders, as leaning posts for small moths,

our markings smeared in a lop-sided mess;
silent and brooding at the worst of times,
noisy and unkempt at best.

Still, they let us fly and cling,
sooth the fire in our heads.
Expecting nothing in return

steer us away from shadow figures,
the false testimony of broken people
who promise everything
at a price so crushing—

shelter us from jagged-edged gaslights
littered with half-dead, broken butterflies,

guide us across cold landscapes
distorted beyond recognition;
away from hollow-eyed banshees
planting sterile seeds in dust.

Measures of Forgiveness

inspired by Anne Lamott

The best apology is changed behavior
            —Unknown

Trapped in halls of human frailty,
you inch along; rough walls
adhere to blistering skin—reminders
you've been here before,
but won't find an exit.

Ruts dug with tarnished spades fill up with anger,
evaporates, rises again, overflows—
mercies harvested,
forgiveness
pulled out by its roots

and it begins again;
look down the long table,
a yard sale of porcelain hearts,
all cracked,
five cent apologies,
fragile in the hand.
You break it, you buy it,
no longer applies.

My Misuse of Obtuse,
the Disillusionment of Words

Poets tell us of the importance of words,
the heat of them. I wish it weren't true.

I'm of that ilk—spinning out on the wrong word,
definitions stuck in traffic on Blunder Road,
mental GPS out of date, spoonerisms, malaprops,
senior moments fight head and mouth for parking space,
unintentionally *obtuse*—

a word, by the way, I misused
the other day on Facebook.
the word intended: *obscure*
hid behind a misty map of detours,

travelled with slip of key-stroke
to Alphabet Avenue—closed for repairs;
language, tired of waiting for a green light,
guns it, word police in hot pursuit;

the voice inside my head grinds out:
make a U-turn when possible—
points out that one rogue comment
shoved into a ditch by one gangly phrase
in too much of a hurry.

And I, driving against the drain surge of
a watered down vocabulary, pronounce
an unread apology DOA.

I've ended up insulting a soul,
their memes and posts *abstruse*
but didn't need to know that truth either way,

though not the only one caressing their cranium
over baffling comments, I feel stupid
stalled in the wrong lane of social media's highway,
when all I really want to say is: *Sorry*.

II.
The Enemies We Cannot See

Aletheia Speaks Out

> *Three things can't be hidden for long:*
> *the sun, the moon and the truth.*
> —attributed to Buddha

When I go home to my holy well,
my hair will weave itself into a nest.

I plant birds for the lady next door to marvel at,
though birds frighten me and say so.

I love to throw myself against walls of mirrors,
see a thousand heads, all agreeable and in love.

What happens in the shadows? You'll have to ask
the other one, the one without feet.

Oh, how she loves curves and angles scattered and warped.
Straightening out her handiwork is so tiresome and best
done in the desert—less distractions.

Goddess of Lies—calm your tornado of sticks.
Throw away the pointed hat.

Call my pretty name and I shall answer—an obedient dog
hoping to chase a bone, but instead,
you toss the horn of truth downstream,

jump in and swim against everything good,
pretend to drown before you'd hug any righteous coastline.

To be foot-less, yet have a foothold on so many souls
frustrates the Hades out of me.

Any time someone asks for the truth, I tell them;
but it's seldom the answer they're looking for.

*Aletheia: The personified spirit of truth

Narcissists Tripping the Light Fantastic

What do they see in the mirror?
Mornings reflecting
    a love misplaced,
or nights, when darkness begs
    for belief in any light?
    Ignoring shadows cast
until the one injury that never was—
    do the mind's fabrications
    line up with the image?

Do they toast themselves
    raising mirrored chalices?
Hope pleasantries stolen
    add up to hearts and flowers?
When did we become instruments
measuring their worth,
    how grateful we should be,
or else?

I stopped wondering about motive.
    It's all about timing—
learned responses replicated on cue.
    The mirrored ball twirls
ballet of distorted light bounces out of tune.
    Sit and watch.
Fear and anger
    love to tango.
Shame and denial
    choreograph an amazing dance.

Fear the Walking Dead

Narcissists are the true zombies of the world.
—from *Malignant Self-Love* by Sam Vaknin

If we smear
blood on our faces
will they shuffle
their horror stories towards different cities?
Lamprey themselves onto victims
who, like them, suffer cravings
never satisfied?

If part of Z Nation,
we'd be their cure—
eager to find
and pick our brains,
they'd follow us
anywhere.
Instead, we give them mercy.

Hunting Instinct

The lion is the most handsome
when looking for food.
—Rumi

They're always the same faces,
same Jacks dealing the same game
in different suits, different hands
shuffling between the shallow
of everyday and elusive
myth of possession,

poets and liars,
intent on devouring
those who promise
mementos
etched in fear;

their seed travels
in secret families,

twisting fate,
stepping over
all lines of sand
that separate fact from fiction.

An archetype unto themselves,
they create their own missions—

and for this
they have chosen you,

because
you scorch
the edges of their vision,
because
you are there.

CFB Trenton, Hermit's Hill: The Piercing

1.
Wanda's getting her ears pierced—
wants me to go with her.
Begs me to take her over the *hill*.
I'll ask my parents.
Sure sweetie they'll say.

Walking back over Hermit's Hill
Wanda's smile is brighter than her gold studs.
She's never been to the top—a longer journey home.

We stroll up arm in arm chatting—seventh grade gossips,
make up new tales to tell her dad.
He loves our elephant jokes.

From the top we hear
my neighbour's blue tick hound
bay at rabbit scent.

Sharing this special place—
we point to my home,
meander through the old orchard,
wonder if the hermit worked this grove.

No one eats the apples now
and there's too many
for wildlife to finish off.

2.
I can't go.
Dinner's at five.
No exceptions.

I'm fire, fangs and tears.
They've known for two weeks
and I'd promised to take her over the hill
but arguing the point is dangerous.

She'll set off up the knoll on her own,
kick at apples
strewn across the ground,
weave-walk through lines
drawn by trees, serenity broken
by the sudden staccato of red-winged blackbirds.

But she has a ways to go.
She drops the apple.

3.
Wanda sits on her porch steps,
eyes dark and dull.
I warn her—
the visit by police,

I'm to find out
what happened and by whom.
She begins to shriek—
runs back in the house.

Her mother spits poison.
I'm no longer welcome.

4
I walk up and across the Hill.
Whatever took place
disintegrates—
fruit rotting in the duff.

5.
Wanda stares through the wire fence.
I'm on the other side of an empty space.
It's two years since last we spoke.
Her voice a cave without echo—
my father is missing.

He's found on a gravel road,
car windows, exhaust pipe
covered and sealed.

No Safe Harbour

Waves of rhythmic battering
   have left her waterlogged,
      yet she continues to resurface
         bobbing with the current.

He has ripped her sails,
   torn her rudder
      from its stern
         til she can no longer manoeuvre;
      compass washed overboard,
   without hope of protection
from the elements

she has learned to feel comfort
   in the certainty of his storm fronts,
      can predict his weather patterns,
         recognize the calm before the storm.

With no visible landmarks,
   no horizon in sight,
      she's forgotten how to navigate.
         He has swallowed all the stars.

Fishing Derby

Said it yourself—
you really don't care,
so we no longer take the bait.
Fish thrown back wait in the reeds,
find we're not alone, none of us that hungry,
we've learned to spot the hand-made flies.

You'll snag yourself eventually,
trophy days over.

For now you bait your hook
catch fish quite beautiful, gleaming.
Some of us feisty and colourful,
some soft with a gentle glow,
some thankful you've offered to clean
their gills, latch on satisfied,
as long as they ignore the barbs.

There's always a lure, *something* to dangle.
You haven't yet hooked a creature
large with teeth, so for now—
Sunday fishing trips, quiet ponds.

What if the next sharp-eyed fish reeled in
bites through your line,
joins our school;
all of us hook-damaged
ghosting through reeds?

Yes, keep fishing.
It's not a safe place to swim.

Lady of the Flies

As flies to wanton boys are we to the gods.
They kill us for their sport.
         —Shakespeare, *King Lear*

Is that when the wounding began? Bullied
by political fiction, searing sub-text behind each chapter,
violent rendition of good old boys left on their own,
painted faces setting off the hunger behind the hunt.
Did you feel left out, denying the thrill, dying to join in?

Was it a shock,
imagining the havoc wreaked subtle and slow,
unclear which side?—*are you Jackie or Ralphina?*
Silencing anyone who knows what beast
rises in tune with the wind.

That irritating wisdom, its acrid vapour blinding—
the message not received. But it'll make a good story
told as easily as picking up a rock.

The flies bow
all buggy-eyed, wings all-a-rub,
unchallenged the *why* gets dirtier over time.
Downturned scar with teeth swallows the light.

The sadness we fold and tuck away—
there must be a reason for picking up the same killing rock,

hammering injuries into our sorrow,
embracing the shards.

Is it like spinning atop a cold sill
on verge of window drop?
Innocence shattered, anguish, rage, revenge—
one colossal hand suspended midair. The surprise,
the fear in those compound eyes as it slams down.

Do you smell it?
It's not cologne.
It's the scent of carrion.

Caught in Celluloid

Now playing: *All About Eve*;
oozing out across stage and screen
minus credits, performed
with dramatic irony in a playhouse where
buttered up popcorn goes bad,
our spirits dragged down sticky aisles.

Eve fashioned from broken ribs,
glitter-glued to city slickers
stuck in a land of make-believe,
that need for applause, like *waves of love*
pouring over footlights—someone else's story acted out.

There's so much to learn;
but her character never does.
Instead, rewrites vacant plots,
aimed at trusting fans who believe
those rehashed monologues.

The bumpy night: expected.
But not the feeling
we're remnants
in a haunted theatre
trapped once the doors close.

Frida

We are but one.
You are many canvasses,
stuck-on landscapes,
brown-eyed, single-browed portraits,
backward spiral of self
holding monkeys,
the fine art of pain
you exploit and repeat,
all dressed up
waiting to hurt.

I feel your loss.
All women
have felt your pain
but our wardrobes are limited,
our men
do not paint murals;
instead we paint on many faces,
pluck our eyebrows.

We are a silent gallery.
No art forms
here. No patrons
lined up for private showings.
We move our pain around
check our losses
at the door.

Confessions of an Alice Munro Character

Somehow, forgot my place.
Born and raised to fit nowhere in particular.
A spectator within the realm of everyone else's destiny—
imagine banding together:
personae embracing our commonalities.
But who was I kidding—
I'm a half-baked fantasy
fed complimentary crumbs, favours
that leave a bad taste in my mouth.

This is what happens when you consider yourself
more than a character in a story.
At least the geography is right and ripe:
a gothic tale set in Ontario's southwest.
You hear trains; track speech patterns within
rural scenes, audible even in the suburbs.
Here, as narrator, I struggle to make sense
of my world, but Alice has the final word
and no one is the wiser.

Sometimes I forget I am a living shadow,
a colourful one, but a shadow all the same.
Almost believe I belong. Almost—
until that certain uncertainty slams into me,
runaway caboose racing in the wrong direction.
Can't seem to get through my head,
nothing is really going to happen.
No matter how many re-writes, my plot is secondary,
my story's title: *waiting for the splash*.

All this shedding light burns holes
in my heart. It is Alice, the omniscient child
with magnifying glass torching a single ant.
Relentless revelations hack away at this
repetitive reminder of what will never be,
yet still I cling to something that lasts the least.

Alice, release me from this ordinary life
you insist is touchable and mysterious.
Separate me from narratives I cannot retrace without
remorse,
or at least, silence the grinding monotony of trains.

A Literary Conspiracy, Figuratively Speaking

The goddess of memory calls
upon her poetic brood, their absentminded aunt:

Touch her lightly on the shoulder,
while she's in the middle of life,
both hands full;
when she's ready to write it down—
Suck it up. Flat-line it. Leave her clutching
woolly afterthoughts. Spinning

around the corner from the commonplace,
bump her into dialogues
where she keeps missing the point.
Syntax scrambling to move forward—
catch her propositioning a preposition,
accuse her under a little-used article:
practicing poetry without a licence.

Hardly aware
she's monitored by her modem,
stick her in a list-serv with no threads
encrypt her web page with passwords
too prosaic; lose her
in the order of things spinning.

Too obscure? she says. That's good!
With no essay in sight,
pondering content over craft,

tired of spinning yarns
under current rules of engaged poetics,
she'll refuse to decipher her own revisions.

Without missing a beat
call in angry herds of iambic pentameters,
rushing through lines of alliteration,
they can reiterate—nothing's free—
it's all in the technique.

Then, if she masters the art of revolution,
tell her she's spinning in the wrong direction.

Musings

In search of pain
he cuts off her hands,
places them atop each other on the mantel
a gesture of patience, yet she notices
an occasional twitch, fingertips itching to get down,
thumb through subversive literature.

    How small, he muses,
    like the hands in cummings' poem.

Yes, I love that poem too. She sighs,
wipes away his bloody tears,
opening her own wounds—
the sting of a single gesture.
In return, he leaves her stained,
arms tattooed with words she can't pronounce.

She senses her Muse approaching—
searches for a pen.
Her toes do not reach the table.
Her own tears cannot peel back the tape
now fastened over her mouth.

The Muse is amused.
Always giving up something for nothing
Not one to think ahead, are you?

Now thought is all she has left,
snarling thick with teeth and spittle,
ideas circle attracted to the scent of pain,
with names familiar as her own family's
and just as unreachable,
the only thought she is now able to grasp.

Ambushed

I walk within labyrinths
of seashore, woodland, desert, plain.
I'm no one's lamb.

My head a windstorm,
my heart a wave that curls,
crests, caves in, batters
sand and rock with equal force,
pulls away, moon-called.

Your eyes dull with disdain, follow me,
ignore   follow   ignore.

I'm sick of these meaningless manoeuvres.
But there's always another wave,
and another, and another.

There's always a lone sniper,
scope out, rifle ready,
and I refuse to call in reinforcements.

I have no interest in your battles.
Come close, reveal yourself,
save us all some time.

What's Cooking? (Cooking Up a Storm)

The voice from across the table
offers an iced-up charcuterie board—
assorted complaints not proffered in peace.
I decline the jam,
the overcooked flesh cut on a bias,
push away the word salad,
refuse to accept her half-baked pie as my own.

It rings a dinner bell in my head—my kid,
roiling at me with a similar menu.
What's eating him?
Throws finger foods in my direction,
complains about the service;
feeds me an elaborate entrée he insists
I've arranged on a dirty platter.

Guilt's grey rabbit slow-cooks in his mouth,
its turbulent stream overflows the pot—
what's he cooking up?
Something you can't serve to guests
but I'll chew on anyway,

and in a flash—I'm back—
the same burnt pan, grey rabbit—
what's she cooking up?
Something I'm unable to swallow
and why is everything cold?

Rug Stains

We all demand to be heard.
Our stories, our lives flow: red wine,
diverse grapes, sundry vineyard locales,
climate unpredictable.

But there's always those careless spills
staining rugs in dissimilar rooms,
creating circular patterns, erratic splotches—
commonplace over continual viewing.

Some clean up with elbow grease and seltzer.
Others: easy cover-ups— wood-heavy,
grain-stressed facades resting on stubborn stains
refusing to fade.

Some are obvious no matter where you stand.
Each discolouration—soiled with narratives
everyone talks about, we try to ignore.

Time chimes in, marks a call for change—
rugs rolled up tossed curb-side.
Will we be more careful with their replacements
or do we laminate these rooms?

Indiscretions wiped away,
failings soaked up,
disposed of quick as the flick of a garbage lid.

Sweeping dirt into corners,
over time we forget
grime climbs walls.

A Litany of Curses for Everyday Assholes

May they always be late for school, for work,
for last call, for every deadline,
always lose their place in books, conversations, in line;
lose every game, every job, their voice, their nerve.

May they be bombarded with bushels of teddy bears
all plush and smiley, each time they open a door.

May they always radiate an unpleasant odour,
sniff a rancid phantom scent,
and drive themselves nuts looking for it.

May herds of lipstick-wearing, cologne-drenched grandmas,
chase them down daily demanding hugs and kisses.

May their houses stink, their kids reek, the stench keep
them up nights washing clothes, bed sheets, towels,
May they be unable to keep anything
clean: the house, yard, the car, themselves.

May unicorn piñatas show up out of nowhere,
showering them with sticky candy hearts and rose petals.

May their parents be filthy rich and disown them,
their spouses have sex with anyone but them.
May their kids hate them, friends betray them,
babies scream at the sight of them.

May the song, *It's a Wonderful World*,
run through their heads non-stop every morning.

May TVs turn off, refrigerators heat up,
computers and cars break down within 10 feet of them.
May animals run away or attack,
flowers wither and die as they walk by.

May they struggle to breathe
in a pool of tears that never evaporates.

May they be wing-slapped by angels,
until they see stars.

Dead Man Walking

He wakes up at autumn's hour

falling
  from a bitter bed, surrounded
    by strangers thin as leaves,

dark as November afternoons;

their crackling speech
  enters the blood,
    cruel capsules

prescribed
              as endless
             repeats
               streaming arterial messages

through a heart set to pass;
                     spat out
 like a sour child
  named after fear
   this ailing spirit
                   crumbles
into a madness,
  thick-coming,
    an immeasurable ceaseless channel,

shore-less as sand
  in a timepiece,
     turned at the precise moment
                    time runs out.

Wear and Tear

My body has always been a challenge,
a womb with its own agenda
reproducing more blood than bodies
miscarriages of justice
ceramic hip a ball and chain
frees me, walks me into a new life,
left hand shakes up my dopamine world
shouldering a drop in memories
scavenger hunt for words
the poem in my head pronounces
accents on all the wrong syllables
a balancing act I'll lose in the end
so don't make me laugh
I can't afford to dribble
I'll be drooling soon enough.

An Irrational Fear of Citrus Preserves

(*with apologies to marmalade lovers*)

Consider the kumquat,
fruit best eaten whole;
more work than pleasure,
relentless jawing
to find that precarious balance—
tart to sweet, pulp and juice:
sour blend of beauty only skin deep,
holding-cell for noxious seeds,
one's mouth must improvise ways,
means for their tedious removal;

a marmalade self-contained,
well-suited to that same-named bitter goop,
for the mere thought of a Dundee jar
makes me pucker. Robertson's *gollywog*—
a bad memory ingrained.
Whose idea stuffing quince, kumquat, grapefruit,
lemon, lime and orange into jars?

From quince to orange from Spain to Scotland,
forced on children through Paddington Bear,
supposedly loved by Victorian spinsters,
widows retiring to Sunday parlours,
their seemingly favourite treat spooned
over bland digestive wafers, scones—

hard-tacked merchant marines forced
to eat this spreadable *Buckley's* in lieu of fruit,

yet this acerbic freak of jams survives,
slathering into the 21st century;
and upon reaching the throes of middle age,
find myself checking
the hands on my epicurean clock,
fearing I will soon wake up
with an unexplainable craving
for toast and marmalade.

MRI: My Photogenic Brain Makes Good

Noisy bang-bang
a room renovation at high speed
nothing like *Grey's Anatomy*.
After it's over I ask to see my brain on screen
the magnetic blend of shadow and light
how my icing-piped squiggles twist and turn
like a California highway
how grey/white matter telescopes
then   bursts into kaleidoscopic
dance routines without the help
of sugar plum fairies
but though miraculous
doesn't show how
before you know it
neurotransmitters
strike a nerve   *or don't*
neurons talk it up   *or don't*
decipher knee-jerk reactions
interpret stove top fingers
soured milk   screams
from high-pitched kids
and what the hell am I looking at—
oversees heartbeats   broken hearts
or should   the brain waves
to a butterfly stomach
intestinal contractions signal back
or don't   prepared for any danger—
dinosaurs, hyenas, spiders   *maybe*
the urge to hunt for a refrigerator

and not eat daffodils
how even now   focused
on my self-taught typing skills
spelling from memory   faulty grammar
hauled across this page   *almost* simultaneously
my fingers search for keys   words   syntax
but what's truly amazing—
remaining perfectly still
in a tube   without the urge to urinate
or scratch my nose for 30 minutes straight.

A Case of Parkinson's During the Pandemic

noun verb   black out
is this the silence   of dopamine?
toilet paper stuck on a shoe   waiting
   for your name to be called

I can't
    articulate this loss   for words   state of emergency
no panic button provided   brain chemicals doing
    their thing   dopamine changes   quick as a hand
    tremor

is this what I want   gambling with brain waves
close to crapping out   the pressure of needing more
    messing me up   this hologram of crazy   not fitting
    anywhere   in any convoluted wasteland

dopamine talk   lyric phrase fail   tongue fizzle-out
pronunciation compress/decompress   dust in my head
gibberish   crammed into ebony fields   nothing
    growing today   perhaps tomorrow   perhaps

    I need a 5 o'clock glass of wine
by 4   some blues
    to bail me out of this   dopamine fog
this half open book

my gray matter sound-room   begging
    for noise-cancelling ear-buds   care package deliveries
    to satisfy my hunger   for touch   travel
asiago cheese.

Heeding the Signs

As kids, we believed a *wire hand*
lived in basement storage rooms—our apartment building
    myth.
Who knows who made it up—grown-ups or us?
a warning to keep us safe, made-up entity
keeping us out of mischief.

Our parents' major rule: stay away from the creek.
The *wire hand*: always illusive—up to no good.
The creek: always there—we saw the changes,
drying trickle to bloated, mud-grey roar.
We warned ourselves to be careful, told tales of rats as big
    as cats.
We never saw one—but knew if cornered they'd go for the
    throat.

There are so many signs warning us keep off the grass
no passing no left turns don't feed the ducks don't feed
    the bears
beware of rip-tides deep end no diving no fishing
    no swimming
beware of flash floods beach closed due to e coli after eating
wait an hour before entering the water—a fallacy
that sat with us for years, like a heavy meal.

I've swum alongside barracuda, snorkeled in shark-infested
    seas.
Treading water—watched man o wars drift by ·
their stinging truth, invisible. Kept my distance
knew the consequences—not believing
what we can't see.

Evenings in Costa Rica, Coco Cliffs, floating
in the pool I search for Mars.
There isn't any threat here that I can see
no god of war heaving spears towards me from above.
The grass and beyond—scorpions spiders snakes.

There's always danger venturing into places
where we know there's pain, a chance
we'll cut our own throats,
wire hand grabbing us from behind,
rats closing in.

The Enemies We Cannot See

Stephen Tait: 1983-2012, from a fentanyl overdose.

By night, his enemies feasted on his heart, like flies
sensing death. His flesh, a winter tree

covered in snow, the wet cold part of him now part of me.
His enemies drain my blood, as they murder him slowly.

Our enemy deals us a hand of black hearts, red clubs
    bashing
blindly, jokers wild, queen face down in sorrow.

His sun dimmed by powder and tinfoil
a slow sinking into bleak horizons, killing our joy.

He is spread out and shining, his enemies slice into him
    like bread,
feed him back to me on a slab.

I want to lift him back up,
but my hands are tied, my back broken.

His death cuts into me. Out pours ooze, nameless and grey,
but there's a light his enemies forget to swallow.

I close my eyes.
The thought of his heart blinds me.

III.
Collision Course

Overwhelmed by the Overwhelm

It's that cliché—a deer on the road,
or cartoon eyes stretching out of your head,
life speeds up,
you're in a tailspin rushing
down a drain of deadlines,
must do's needle you from behind,
cattle-prod ribs and thighs,
timings off
as you slap away the wind.
One shoe, glued to the floor
gums up time-frames.
A voice, shrill inside your skull
bounces out accusatory reverb
at the exact moment giant shadows
surround you, belting out time-sensitive
questions you've forgotten
the answers to, but knew last week.
In slow motion
you melt—a pool of molasses
staring at the ceiling.
It's a new day,
the deer the headlights
cartoon eyes popping
and everything moves forward

except you.

Chaos

Hunts at forest edges;
can't enter unless invited,
as said of vampires.

Beckons glib and smug;
Come play with me. Let me in.

Pine needles drop, leaves
curl with every word uttered.

We've lost count—the souls lost or afraid,
the dead and dying,—but not this one.
This one counts them all.

We're blinded,
our mourning so dark
we invite it in.

Relying on our kindness,
colourless creature slithers before us,

between, behind, inside us.
Black brackish eye at the back of its neck blinks.
Deserts appear beneath its belly.

Hurricanes fly out of its mouth.
Hearts and knives fall to earth.
We pick up one or the other.

Lost

People ruin beautiful things.
—Kahlil Gibran

We think,
therefore we are full of ourselves.

No longer hear earth's songs
we've forgotten her lyrics.

Barely notice what vibrates,

   what dances around us.

We remain stationary
anchored to the intangible

                      inward   non-place

we've created and called real,

divorced

from the planet we stand on,
all that sustains us.

One Step Closer to the Sun

Glorious rays
disrupt cells
create microscopic monsters.
Stare into that light long enough
all that brightness
parches more than skin,
burns out the eyes.
Without rain or windbreak—
scorch marks,
heat scars.

Thirst unquenched,
nothing cools,
just craving and madness,
no wind or water,
cloud, season, colour,
no movement except towards decay,
a slow feast
before the shrinking stench
hollows out life.

What sound—
except the sting and pop
of slow death,
fire purifying
a sizzling absence—
grey aftermath
begging for rain
and any sudden wind.

Soup

"Soup" is a description given to plastic debris
suspended in the ocean.

man-made soup carried by water and wind, spat
onto beaches—medical waste backdrop tapped, siphoned
    off—
syringes, condoms spent like party favours—

celebratory rubbish for each new year—snake   dragon
horse   monkey, non-degradable annual revelry—
seahorse and elephant's synthetic end sadder than the real
    thing—
Nature's demise—a return, a breakdown cycle of life,
death   extinction accelerated by our love for the
    throwaway—

tossed without ceremony—cluttered cemetery
of idealized coastlines—the fruits of our oil-based labour—
our collective desires—non-recyclable products,

our discarded hearts—landfill escapees nestle
into newfound niches—land and sea,
embellished with artificial blooms—
their flowering time eternal—

sea foam or polystyrene, the romance of salt and sea—
home of whale, salmon, coral reef or cod transformed—
these new denizens: *more than meets the eye* non-action
    figures—

foregone conclusions flung with childhood abandon
into the depths of coastal dumps—
our road to infinity paved with disposable lighters—

mannequin hands shake on empty promises—
a toxic deal sealed in triplicate—
what use medicinal debris, used IVs to a dying sea—
no bottled bleach cleans up after itself—
no tide scrubs clean these ocean floors.

Clandestine Photo Shoot:
Holmes Foundry, Point Edward, Ontario

> *Among the workers exposed for two years or more,*
> *there was a 600% increase in lung cancer,*
> *an 11,000% increase in respiratory disease,*
> *and five cases of mesothelioma.*
> *Women who washed their husbands' clothes*
> *also suffered health effects due to inhalation.*
> —Greg McConkey, *Valley Review June 2, 2019*

Camera's click and whirl is startling on its own,
like disturbed wing flaps collecting air,
quick movements slapping deserted spaces.

Paint spray cans of fallen artists, empty of colour now,
but what they were—hissing hues of mists applied
like the drama of a thrown drink dripping down,
off-colour remarks smacked on poisoned walls tagged
    for demolition.

There is beauty in letters,
a history of tints in distress,
something to say in the dark—
it is almost, always night here.

Even humour permeates these ruins, unintentional art,
a single chair bathed in dusty patches of sunlight,
painted office signs sprayed with tongue in cheek,
the spit of sarcasm drenched in green.

The empty echo of no sound—unnerving, scattered scraps
from vagrants, addicts who have called this place home.
This vacancy cradles a discord of dead voices, whirl of
    machines,
the heat of lethal labour, bark and yell of ghost workers.

Reek of sweat and metal gone,
the walls withstand a noxious history,
venomous worms unseen settle into lungs and lives:
grime no one can wash off or demolish.

Heat Wave

People are burning.
Melting into one scream—
others don't know enough to burst into flame.
Days are burning up hours.
No time heals the slow sear—
all those empty stomachs, scorched hearts.

My life's a controlled burn.
Sleeping seeds erupt, green flourishes
rise up through muck and wasted carbon.

The world is kindling and charcoal.
Embers break off
scarring Earth's face.

We talk about all the suffering souls,
our flora and fauna smouldering—
meme it to cinders, scroll over and dream,
insist our thoughts are with them—
hot air humanity fanning flames in all directions.

The blaze closes in.
We draw the blinds.
It's not our house burning.

I Do Know the Spelling of Money

after Tonga Eisen-Martin's
I Do Not Know the Spelling of Money

Yeah, we've wrapped ourselves up in a new blanket of bullets,
our ancestors emptying rounds into buffalo herds,
presidential parades, the odd protest march.

Someone's always yelling—
Let's build walls.
Let's kill what really matters.

Can't hear cries for peace
amid hot metal outbursts tearing through crowds,
scent of gun powder all the rage for any holiday gathering.

The bullet chamber turns, family trees trimmed
with nooses up in time for Christmas.
In Canada, we've got our own crosses to hide.

White history backwash vomits up:
that's the way it was done; those were the times
when heroes dismantled entire generations.

In this era of statue meltdowns—
I still adore Jackson's hair.

My white feminist confusion doesn't mix
with military-issue fly-by shootings,
fly-by-the-seat-of-our-pickup truck patriotism.

Next to ads sporting two hundred dollar Nikes,
billboards insist *we're all in this together.*
What's in your wallet?

Charity bounces off an empty fridge.
Compassion ricochets off the facade of village figments,
rows of panic rooms where the remote is King.

Love, a surgical mask torn away
takes with it the skin off our lips.

We Do Not Tolerate Difference

after Jericho Brown

We teach anyone different the *shoulds* of our lives—
School-marm bully-sticks whacked across knuckles.

Across knuckles anxiety bleeds—ours not theirs—
pushed into corners, dunce cap forced on heads.

Stories told after church, forced on heads,
from the caves of our mouths spitting it all out.

Spitting it all out—our filth
we don't want wiped off; convinced they'll wear it as their
own.

They'll wear as their own what belongs to them, as they
always have.
Not interested in anyone's hand-made crown of thorns.

Our crown of thorns, poison-dipped they've throw down,
grand inquisition shaken off like the spit.

They've had enough.
We've taught them the *shoulds* of their lives.

Poem Written by a White Woman

Blackness in the white imagination
has nothing to do with Black people
—Claudia Rankine

August—reading Poem-a-Day
supporting the June protests, Black Lives Matter.
My words wormhole into long excuses—
I'm walking on soft boiled eggs.
Pulled towards a movement that's always been there;
realize I've never paid attention to the glory songs,
the gospel truth.

Hanging onto threads of history black and strong,
can't stop showing off my lack of insight.
My ignorance forms questions:
What can I say? How do I say it?
But it's time to listen.

Skinned, white-knee privilege—painless
next to sunlit nightmares, night time
brutality invades homes, streets,
neighbourhoods, everyday violence
seeps into closed eyes and ears.

My own knowing curls up in disbelief
empathy useless, a cloudy glass
full of water I'll never drink.

Some days, the eggs I walk on break
though hard boiled.
I spend mornings listening,
reading poems—lives I'll never touch.
There's a siren in the background,
in my head.

Today I walk on raw eggs.
I don't complain.

Land of Confusion

What if all is lost and it's supposed to be?
The revelation of Revelations as the new Genesis,
the chaos, God prepared for all along.

Jesus, I don't talk to you as often as I should.
When I do it's easier in a language
I don't understand, but you do.
All may be lost, but we won't fault ourselves,
we'll blame your Father, our Father.

Since the garden we've allowed everything
to proceed towards a noisy abyss,
our pride always the main course,
craving dessert before our daily bread.

Before the first bite, you knew we'd mess up.
We'd fight for the last piece of pie.

Jerome's tweezers broken,
Androcles dead and gone,
there are too many lions with thorns in their paws
not enough Daniels to go around.

The World Gone Viral in Five Parts

i. submission calls for poems about the virus

We've been asked to write about *It*,
like a patriotic duty dedication to the essentials,
the front-liners running the show for us,
signs of empathy for the dead, dying, those suffering.

Submission calls—
a call to wear masks, wash hands, stay home.
How's your isolation going?

Compassion reminders
wavering before all *this* happened
may return to its spotty existence—
once this virus goes back to sleep.

ii. home & garden

My husband travels now
within the confines of our yard,
curb-side pick-ups,
window/phone visits with mom,
neighbourhoods quarantined to house & garden
like the magazine—look,
don't touch and can't afford.

He edges our gardens to the unique
timing of song sparrow,
cardinal's laser cowboy calls,
finches chatter, pepper their gossip
with *Reeeeallly,* demands of *Squeeeze Meee.*

When weather evens out
we physically-distance ourselves,
drink in hand, coolers ready
for brief two meter encounters;
far enough away, yet close enough
for quick bathroom trips home and back.
Missing families, friends, even with outdoor visits,
conversing through media—it's not enough.

iii. home and beyond

During sun's unbalanced appearances,
we stroll through the neighbourhood, wave and talk—
people we've never seen in all our years here.

Nature trails fill up with masked characters, their pets.
We play human dodge ball. Zigzag for the sake of health.

I'm left empty by these moments of freedom.
My connections with flora and fauna disjointed
the lack of privacy distracting.

Indoors, windows closed,
there's silence's soft ring.

For some, this explosion of quiet is welcome,
there are souls praying for five minutes of peace,
others: the isolating hush clouds uncertain minds.

Machine clatter, vehicle rumblings
blanket the air with absence—
replaced by the territorial banter of birds.

Their orations clear the air; remind me how
unnecessary we are.

iv. beyond ourselves

Without us, Nature relies on nothing but itself,
the earth's rotation, the availability of a sun.

Even Covid finds a niche,
perhaps back to its roots, undisturbed,

dancing on the backs of bats,
pangolin scales, not bothering anything,

maybe a casual visit by bacterial hosts,
swapping soup recipes with primordial ooze,

playing hide and seek with other viral entities,
none of us around to disturb the balance of life,
disrupting animal kingdoms.

Vegetation, tree roots choking out
deserted factories, our useless dwellings
swallowed up by unstoppable beauty.

v. lest we forget

In our house we drink wine,
listen to music, solve jigsaw puzzles,
and amuse ourselves.

Nursing homes, hospitals
would welcome anyone solving
this pandemic puzzle, corking this
viral overload or doing anything amusing.

The ICU listens to a different silence.

Nothing avian about this quiet—broken by
monitors' beeps and tweets, ventilators'
inhale hiss   exhale sigh.

No banter, visitors' worried questions.
No patient complaints, repeated buzzers
demanding pillows, bed pans, pain killers.

Cries for help muffled by sedation, machine hook ups,
long drones of fear, isolation and stopped hearts.
Medical staff drowning in a sea of code blues.

Social Media Hegemony

Love bombed in all the wrong news feeds
hacked identities forward messages: want you to share.
You've got 24 hours to lip sync a storm—
Tik tok, tik tok. *Un-friend, block, delete.*

What lurks behind the unknown profile?
Clicking on nightshade's shadow dance
it's a mushy eggplant gif—no envy here, no *Haha, Wow.*

We're pickled pink, and on that sour note,
trolls corner the market on vinegar by the bin.
Spreading the virus everyone's searching for
if cornered: false news, YouTube videos
fill the airwaves—comments disabled.

Scrolling rivers of posts meant to inspire,
congratulations replaces kindness,
the opinionated chastised, emails, texts ignored,
tweet 280 characters of free speech or f-off,
instagram photos reach the usual twenty-five.

Emoji hearts show up at odd hours, way past their bedtime.
I may know you beyond the keyboard, the avatar.
So I've built a fort out of poetry books.
Update myself lobbing lines, stanza and verse.

It's okay to suffer in cyberspace—all the memes say so—
anything that matters melting away on empty links.

Facebook heroes posting cats below caring emoticons,
all those *thumb ups* waiting to be born.

Long notes composed for *like/love* responses;
accused of leading an armchair life by *friends*,
beyond-reproach-ethics favour the intellectual muscle
behind the 'right' people thinking differently;
different people speaking up—how dangerous is that?

Social media hash tags itself—you're it!
There's a new Eggplant King smelling up the internet.

Devalued and Discarded
—Thanks for the Memories

It was nothing personal.
We were thought to be dying trees,
the wrong species in a long
ridge of *lovers and good friends.*

In spite of torn out pages, broken branches,
we glue ourselves back together,
scarring up beautifully;

our inflorescence
thunderous in tone, primed
in loud, burning hues,
opaque and dimming shades—
we know where we stand,
who we are.

There'll always be *someone,*
something bathing
in a sea of dead wood,
destined to fertilize
what can't be killed.

Sensory Overload, Echolocation in for Repairs

If I can believe my eyes—it's late.
I can't visualize this heart pain,
or so my woman-clock articulates,
its fine-tuned fork chiming
beat-ups per minute.

Did I hear you correctly?
Echolalia's long drip
convulses through imaginary pools.
I smell the quack of controversy
from here/hear/there,

the pitter-patter of its webbed feet,
geese in formation
honking up the wrong tree
makes my ears weep.

Heartbreak shows up in this poem:
a low frequency ping,
a mispronunciation,
its sour stink glides by so close—
you cannot not taste it.

Odium flails its wings in all directions.
Caught in its stone-toothed trap
ego feathers up,
you stay, me go.

Strange echoes touch me.
Swans—their love-dance plays on my fingertips.
They trumpet a song, one about a mermaid
who learns to swim
through fire.

Scattered Seed (Going Against the Grain)

The times we're stuck and want to be—
resist ideas of change, hard labour,
dragging ourselves through earth, pushing
against stony ground, not knowing what's ahead,
seeing a clear view of what's left behind,
plowed under, basking in cool sticky mud
seems comfortable, permanent.

We hold on, or like seeds we are scattered—
pressed into rows of indented soil—
falling in line alongside fellow seedlings
close enough to touch.
Cultivation depends on so much,
sun, soil and weather.

Some of us, taken by wind
fall on hard land, ill-suited,
find nowhere to grow sturdy, deep roots impossible,
or we ground ourselves in fallow fields,
flourishing glorious and alone,

but some of us tumble towards flowering meadows,
hue-driven, wild, and as we blossom
petals reach out, ready
to hear our stories,
touch our differences.

Just a Note to Say

Thank you.
What a surprise!
How kind and thoughtful.

The wrapping paper: flowers, trees,
ghost eyes leering through leaves—beautiful.

Trussed up with pink and blue ribbons—
change to black when no one's watching.
It's the prettiest box of darkness I've ever received.

The timing was perfect: delivered
while I danced with sunbeams.

Only you would have thought of that!

Wish I could've kept such a wonderful gift,
but your shadows begged for release.

Rather than re-gift,
I opened the box,
showed them my night dance.

They turned into moon beams
and skipped   across   the stars.

Yawn, Comma, Yawn

after Like, Comma, Like *by Kay Gabriel*

This poem has no context or meaning
slapped to death   schadenfreude buried deep
flipping away from a bitter edge
it has no place   alienable rights
no revenge obsessions to drive home
no puzzles to solve   emotional intelligence
or anything to bitch about.
There are no dragonflies slapping their wings
at the back door of these lines   no sold-out garden
    recitals
no miniscule musicians playing every adagio I dredge up.
Finding reasons for this poem
is like stumbling upon naked strangers
peeking through your neighbour's bushes
under a new moon at midnight.

Let's All Collide

Don't you wish we could empty our thoughts
into black holes, into a universal vacuum
the minuses of the day,
the harmful, trashed and disorderly, swept
up with the sad, the unapproachable, people crossing
lines without shame,

or wish upon all the black holes,
negative starlight imploding into something
lovely and loud, quiet and joyful?

Scientists announce there's been a black hole collision,
another clashing of matter, anti-matter, all lives matter.

Why don't we all collide into one another?
Merge—one gigantic black hole
belonging to a new class—
one new class—one exotic colourful object
instead of separate elements
pushing the universe apart.

NOTES

Various poems in Section I and II are inspired by books on Narcissism and personality disorders including:

Behind the Mask: An Introduction into Covert Narcissism by Ayden Guner

Malignant Self Love: Narcissism Revisited by Sam Vaknin, various websites and articles devoted to people with and affected by persons with NPD (Narcissistic Personality Disorder) including *Psychology Today* and *Quora*.

"Now We are Six": After reading the latest books from the three mentioned writers, meeting them all for the first time on the same weekend, while reading *Tao of Pooh* and *Te of Piglet* by Benjamin Hoff. The line: "A fish can't whistle and neither can I" is from Winnie the Pooh's Cottleston Pie.

"Who Could Try to Tell Us We're Not Beautiful": Title inspired by a line in the poem *Absolute* by Jacqueline Woodson

"The Guitar-Shredder's Ex: *Non Sequitur in E Minor*": Line: "One white duck on your wall." from "One White Duck" by Jethro Tull.

"Caught in Celluloid": title from the song "Carpet Crawlers" from *Lamb Lies Down on Broadway* by Genesis. *All About Eve*: 1950 movie starring Bette Davis and Anne Bancroft. The line: " … applause, like waves of love pouring over footlights" taken from a line spoken by Eve Harrington that begins: "If nothing else there's applause …" Also reference to Bette Davis as Margo Channing's line: "Fasten your seat belts. It's going to be a bumpy night."

"Frida": Artist Frida Kahlo.

"What's Cooking? (Cooking Up a Storm)": Grey rabbit in dream symbolism is considered a trickster, someone who wants to take advantage of you, a symbol of dishonesty.

"Soup": After "Hong Kong Soup 1826" a photo documentary series by Mandy Baker depicting plastic debris collected from over 30 different beaches in Hong Kong since 2012. 1826 is the amount of tonnage. "Soup" is a description given to plastic debris suspended in the ocean—a direct reference to the waste crisis in Hong Kong.

Acknowledgements

A big thank you to Michael Mirolla and everyone at Guernica Editions.

Thanks and Love to my PoGo Girls: Jesse Burnquist, Janice Green, Bernadette Wagner.

The Blue Water Writers.
The amazing Not the Rodeo Poets gang.

The continued support of James Deahl and Norma West Linder, Grace Vermeer, Debbie Hill, Mary Frost, Heather Rath.

Adele, Peggy and John, Hope, Venera, Carman, Pat—you are sorely missed.

Special thanks to Molly Peacock, Patrick Lane (RIP), Stuart Ross, Catherine Owen, Kimmy Beach, Di Brandt, Karen Solie, Lisa Richter, Marj Hahne, Ellen Bass, Marie Howe, Kim Addonizio for their editorial insights, workshops and advice,

and to: Bunny Iskov and The Ontario Poetry Society, Stan, Kevin and London Open Mic, Tom Cull, Karen Schindler and Poetry London, The League of Canadian Poets.

Poems have been published in various versions in the following publications:

Windsor Review, Literary Review of Canada, FreeFall, Quills Literary Magazine, Synaeresis, Quarantine Review, Trinity Review, Poetry||Pause (League of Canadian Poets), Time of the Poet: True North with Canadian Poets & Storyteller (digital), High Shelf (Portland Oregon), Muleskinner (U.S.) And anthologies:

Lummox 7, 8,

Voices in the Darkness Vol. 5 (Burning Effigy Press)

Arborealis (2019 Beret Press)

Shout It Out, Poems Against Domestic Violence (Lost Tower Publications 2016)

Infinite Passages (Beret Days Press The Ontario Poetry Society)

Tamarack, A Canadian Anthology (Lummox Press U.S)

The Banister 2014, 2018, 2020, 2022 (The Canadian Authors'. Assoc. Niagara Branch)

Love Lies Bleeding A Canadian Poetry Anthology 2021, 2022(Beret Days Press)

Beautiful: In the eye of the beholder (Sweetycat Press 2022)

Poetry London Annual Poetry Contest 2021: 3rd Prize: "Sensory Overload Echolocation in for Repairs"; 1st Annual Venera Fazio Poetry Contest 2020:1st Prize: "Clandestine Photo Shoot, Holmes Foundry, Point Edward, Ontario".

The Banister 2022 Vol 37: 1st Prize "CFB Trenton Hermit's Hill—The Piercing.

ABOUT THE AUTHOR

Lynn Tait is a poet and photographer born in Willowdale, Ontario and now resides in Sarnia Ontario with her husband, Rob. She began writing poetry in public school and has not stopped writing since. Her poetry has won, placed and been shortlisted in various contests, published in numerous magazines, journals including *The Literary Review of Canada, Vallum, CV 2, FreeFall* and in over 100 poetry anthologies world-wide. Her photography and digital art has appeared in art literary journals and graced the covers of a least nine poetry books. She is an associate member of the Academy of American Poets, and a full member of The Ontario Poetry Society and League of Canadian Poets. *You Break It You Buy It* is her debut collection, and she is presently working on her second book of poems.

MIX
Paper
FSC® C100212

Printed by Gauvin Press
Gatineau, Québec